You Can, If You Try.

Samantha V. Williams

Contributing authors
Kayla Williams and Isaiah Williams

Illustrator
Taranggana

Editor
Margaret Soleyn

You can, if you try.

by Samantha V. Williams

© 2020 Samantha V. Williams

ISBN: 9798602880489

All rights reserved. No part of this publication may be reproduced, distributed, or transmitted in any form or by any means, including photocopying, recording, or other electronic or mechanical methods, without the prior written permission of the publisher, except in the case of brief quotations embodied in critical reviews and certain other noncommercial uses permitted by copyright law.

A percentage of the proceeds of this book will go towards charitable organizations in St. Vincent and the Grenadines that are commissioned to supporting boys and girls in their development.

" Great story, showing courage and a beautiful heart,
We can all share in friendships, we can all do our part,
Thalia is like many girls her age,
that fear, that shyness, but the effort was made to turn the page.

Believe you can, all you have to do is try,
those were the words of Thalia's mother, it was the truth, it was no lie,
So although she was criticized by the group of kids,
Courage arose, although to play with them, they had forbid.

On the beach, as the sand castle grew more and more,
the kids noticed something amazing in Thalia, something beautiful for sure,
even Trey had to admit that what she was doing was unique,
and there it had begun, friendships that will last longer than the day, longer than the week.

A wonderful addition yet again to Samantha's growing literary endeavours,
As she explores friendship and courage for readers present and future,
It will help to teach and enlighten children, especially those who are shy,
So let's all get ready for "You can if you try!"

Rick Francis - Author

Dedicated to my mom, siblings and children.

Once upon a time in a very scenic village called Harmony Vale there lived a quirky 9-year-old girl named Thalia. She had sparkling hazel brown eyes, mahogany brown hair, glowing caramel complexion and though it was rarely seen she had a smile that brightened the world. Thalia attended the nearby school with the other children in the village but spent a lot of time by herself. Sadly, most of her days at school she was unhappy because the children were unkind to her. The fact is Thalia was small in comparison to other children her age and this made her painfully shy.

She also appeared weird to them because she enjoyed exploring the outdoors whenever she could, satisfying her curiosity about the animals and insects that live amongst us but often go unnoticed, like her.

Thalia lived with her loving mom, Juanita, who was unaware of her daughter's feelings of insecurity. To her, Thalia was the most perfect little girl in the world; she was beautiful, smart and kind. Undoubtedly, Juanita's love for Thalia outnumbered the stars in the sky. Thalia felt the same about her mother too.

They were poorer than most people in Harmony Vale, but Juanita worked very hard, making sure they always had what was needed. Their home was a tiny well-crafted wooden house that was painted green and stood on the top of the highest hill in that village. The size of the house was a perfect fit for both of them, and the location gave them a panoramic view of neighbouring communities and a fantastic view of the sea that was only minutes away. Thalia and her mother took great pleasure in going to the sea on weekends, but sometimes when Mom had to work she allowed Thalia to go to the bay with strict instructions to stay on the shore. And though she would be tempted by the crystal clear water inviting her to come in for a swim, she never ever disobeyed.

The sea was Thalia's favorite place to be. She enjoyed the sound of the waves rolling onto the beach, the seagulls' screams, splashing around in the water and sometimes just chilling under the shade of the almond trees. She also loved exploring and while at the sea, which the villagers referred to as the bay, she would walk slowly along the shore looking for seashells that looked different from the others. In a very comforting way the shells, in their uniqueness, reminded her that she too was special.

It was Friday, the last day before school closed for summer vacation and she was happy. This meant that she could go to her favourite place in the world as often as she wanted. The first weekend was awesome. Thalia's mom packed a picnic basket and the two of them enjoyed the entire Saturday at the bay. The rest of the weekend was perfect too even though they just played board games. Their time together always warmed her heart. This was a welcomed escape from what she was feeling.

Monday was fast approaching, and Thalia dreaded being left alone during the week after mom left for work. On most days she went to the bay but on others she just sat in her yard staring at the neighbours' children, as they played.

"Why don't you go over there with them and play?"
Her mom would often ask.
The children all went to school together but they always made fun of Thalia because of her size. They always teased and called her names, and never once asked her to come and play. So, Thalia was afraid of what the children might do, or the things that they might say. Thalia never told her mother about what the children did; she didn't want her to worry or feel dismayed. However, her mom saw that her daughter was very sad and lonely, so she always insisted that Thalia try to make friends with the children in the neighbourhood.

Thalia would reply,
"I can't right now, Mom, but one day maybe I will try."
"You can start by just saying hi. You can if you try,"
Mom further encouraged with the most beautiful smile.

Thalia always longed to have a friend, one who would love her for just who she is. It didn't matter if it were a boy or a girl. It wouldn't matter if they were rich or poor, big, small, tall or short. She just wanted a friend who was kind at heart.

One sunny summer morning, after Mom had left for work at the local grocery shop, Thalia got dressed to go to her favorite spot. But upon hearing the loud roaring of laughter she ran out of the house determined not to be stopped. Today was going to be the day she tried. She wanted to play too. "I have to try; I have to try," she repeated in her head as she remembered her mother's word of advice.

So, bravely she stepped, one foot at a time, right foot, left foot, cautious was her stride. Step by step, she walked anxiously towards the children who were playing gleefully. Still, the fear was too much for this shy little girl and she walked back to her home where she sat pouting quietly in the dirt. She felt sad because she didn't try hard enough and before she knew it the day had gone; she didn't realize it until she heard....

"Hi darling, how are you?"
It was the voice of her loving mother. Thalia looked around and saw her mom looking at her with sadness in her eyes, so she faked a little smile and answered, "I am fine."
"What did you do today?" Her mother further probed.
Thalia answered, "I sat in the yard and played. I didn't feel like going down to the bay."

Day after day, Thalia tried...bravely she stepped one foot at a time, right foot, left foot, cautious in her stride. Step by step, she walked anxiously towards the children who were playing gleefully. This went on day after day for two weeks, yet Thalia never made it to the children who played happily.

One night as Thalia and her mother sat staring up at the sky as they normally would do, sensing her sadness Mom questioned,
"What is the matter with you?" "I'm afraid that I won't ever grow big enough or be good enough at anything to do what the other children can so easily do," Thalia replied as she let out a big sigh.
"You can!" answered Mom, who watched her and smiled.
Thalia quickly responded, "Mom, you don't understand. I just can't, it's true. I just can't do what the other children do."
Mom felt hurt by her daughter's self-doubt and thought carefully about her next words. She took Thalia's hands and held them tightly in hers, and told her something she would not easily forget.

And so Mom affirmed, "You can do, anything you put your mind to. You are so special and so smart, Thalia, you have the kindest, purest little heart. Always remember that you have the ability to do anything that you put your mind to. But first, you must believe in you. You must believe that you can, and work at whatever it is you want to do with diligence and determination. Then, I promise, anything in the world, you can do."
Thalia did not respond but thought in her mind that the very next day she was at least going to give it a try.

And so she did. The very next morning when she awoke, she knew what she had to do, so, dressed in her favorite purple sundress with no shoes on her feet, she approached the other children, afraid to speak. A little girl with curly brown hair heard her coming and began to stare. Soon all of the other children stopped playing and gathered around her in a crowd. Thalia looked at the children too scared to say a word especially when she heard, "What do you want?" A little boy was shouting, questioning her, aloud.

He appears to be the leader of the group she quickly thought and stood figuratively shaking in her boot.
"Can I play with you all?" her voice trembled as she muttered those words. She hung her head to the ground playing nervously with her chin, while she stood awaiting their answer, standing motionless, she stood very, very still.

Some of the children said, "No!" while the others stood silent and did not reply. But unhappy with their response, Thalia boldly asked, "Why?" even to her surprise. Shocked at her response, the boy smiled and questioned, "What games can you play? Cricket, marbles? Can you play soccer or dodge ball? Little girl," he said in a mean sarcastic tone,

"You are so small, can you even throw a stone?" Another little boy who was dressed in a shade of blue that was bright joined in and mocked her shouting, "I bet she can't even fly a kite." Holding back tears Thalia courageously replied, "I cannot play marbles, cricket or football. I may not be able yet to fly a kite, but I can if you'll just let me try."

Thalia found out that little boy's name was Trey. She heard the little boy dressed in blue call out his name as he walked away.

Unconvinced by Thalia's pledge to try, Trey replied, "It's useless if you can't already play; we don't have time to show you, so go away, go away!"

And there, all alone Thalia stayed. The seconds seemed like hours as she stood staring at the children, embarrassed at what had just happened. She ran back to her house as fast as she could.

When coincidentally her mom was walking home and saw Thalia running away from the neighbours' children, she hurried home to comfort her daughter with the tightest hug and warmest kiss.

Through her sobbing, Thalia managed to say, "They won't even let me try to play."
"I'm really sorry," said Mom. "Everything will be okay, you will feel better, maybe not right now but soon you will. Their words were unkind, but find it in your heart to forgive them. Please try."
"Why!" exclaimed Thalia. "Why should I?"
Her mother had the kindest heart, so what she said next came as no surprise.
"To forgive them doesn't mean that what they did was okay. It just means you're not going to let those mean things get in your way."

Thalia listened carefully to the words her mother said, and though right now she couldn't forgive those children, in her heart she knew one day she may. The days that followed, Thalia refused to try. Instead, she sat gloomily in her yard watching the ships in the bay as they passed by.

Until...
This one unbelievably beautiful day she decided that she was not going to let their meanness get in her way. And so, off she went to her favorite place in the world, to the seaside went this special, kind, smart little girl. She sat on a rock lost in the beauty of the bay. Then plopped down into the sand and started to play. She started to doodle in the sand; flowers, trees, stick figures of children who appeared to be frolicking in the sea were what she drew.

And as she sat looking up at the seagulls in the sky, in the corner of her eyes she saw two little crabs scampering by. This inspired her to dig, in hopes of seeing more sand creatures, and before she realized it she had dug an enormous hole that was soon filled with water as the waves rolled in. As her feet got wet she decided to go further back from the shore and slowly she started piling sand more and more. And as the hours passed by she discovered that she had made the biggest sandcastle she had ever seen, so to herself she smiled. I didn't know that I could do this she thought; it's good that I tried, she said to herself beaming with pride.

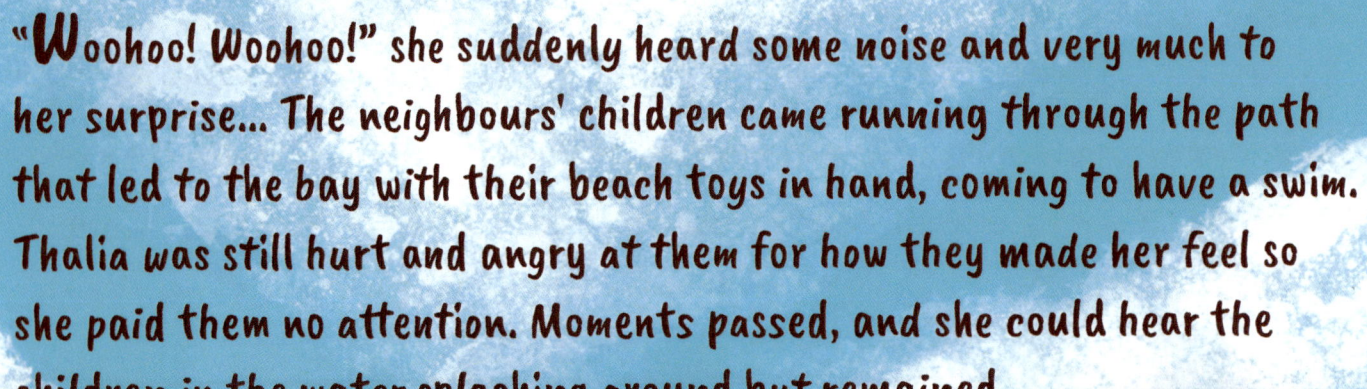

"Woohoo! Woohoo!" she suddenly heard some noise and very much to her surprise... The neighbours' children came running through the path that led to the bay with their beach toys in hand, coming to have a swim. Thalia was still hurt and angry at them for how they made her feel so she paid them no attention. Moments passed, and she could hear the children in the water splashing around but remained focused on her task.

And as she continued to build her sand castle, what she did not hear or see was the little girl with curly hair colored brown stepping, one foot at a time, right foot, left foot, cautious in her stride, step by step she walked anxiously, towards Thalia who was playing all alone quite happily.

Suddenly Thalia noticed a shadow blocking out the light from the sun, looking up, she saw the same little girl from that embarrassing day. The little girl looked down at Thalia, smiling from ear to ear as she asked:
"How did you do that?"
Quite surprised, Thalia couldn't respond. Instead, she just looked up at her. "Come on guys, come and see this. It is just great," invited another little girl in a pretty flowered swimsuit colored pink.

And pretty soon all the children came rushing to see the grand sand castle Thalia had built.
"Wow!"
"How fantastic!"
"Look at that!"
The other children said nothing; they just stood there silently admiring Thalia's beautiful work.

Thalia looking up at the children timidly smiled, when down from a nearby tree Trey climbed.

"I did not know that you could do that," said the little boy who had told her to go away, when all she wanted to do was play.

Thalia looked up at him and replied, "I didn't know I could either until I tried."

She smiled, feeling proud of herself for being kind.

"Can you teach us how to build sand castles too?" asked the little girl with the curly brown hair as she introduced herself.

"My name is Sarah. What's your name?"

"Thalia," she answered without any fear.

Sarah was the first to sit, patiently awaiting sand castle building tips and tricks. Thalia bravely stood and started instructing: "Just think about what you want to design, and you can start building. You already have all the tools right here: sand, water, buckets, shovels, even shells and sticks. You can make your sand castle any way you wish."

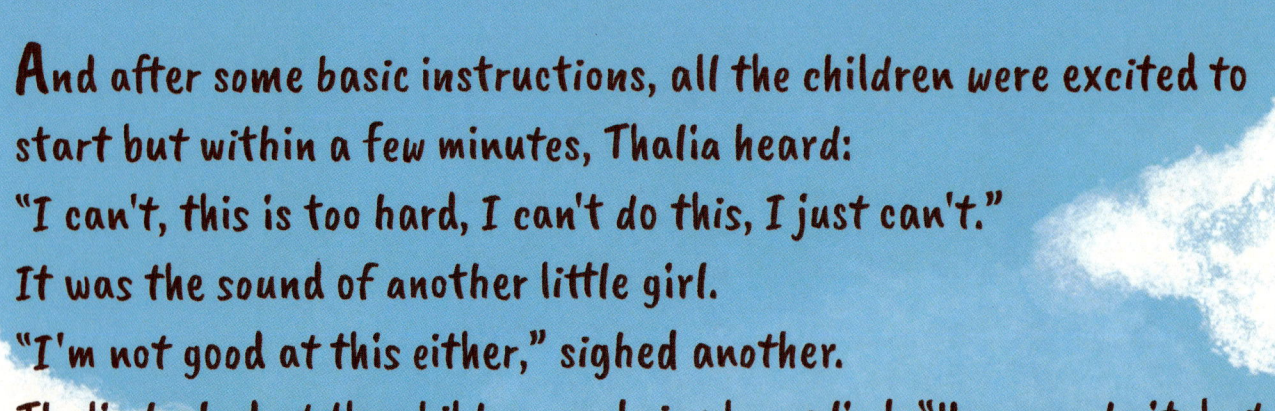

And after some basic instructions, all the children were excited to start but within a few minutes, Thalia heard:
"I can't, this is too hard, I can't do this, I just can't."
It was the sound of another little girl.
"I'm not good at this either," sighed another.
Thalia looked at the children and simply replied, "You can do it, but you must first believe with all of your might that you can then you will, if you just try."

And, soon the beach was filled with sand castles; some topped with shells, others with sticks as flags. No more were the cries of "I can't" only the sight of beautiful sand castles, the results of "I can."

The children were all very pleased and one by one they turned running excitedly into the sea.

Meanwhile, Thalia remembering her mother's rule sat close enough to the sea so the water only washed over her feet. And as she sat looking at the children playing in the water she noticed Trey coming out of the water. He looked puzzled but plopped down beside her and asked,

"Why were you so kind to us when to you we were so mean?"

But before Thalia could speak, he continued,

"I am sorry for the mean things I said and for causing you to cry."

Thalia looked Trey straight in his eyes,

"I forgive you," she said and smiled.

Confident that he had made a new friend, Trey curiously asked, "Did you know that you can do something so amazing?" Thalia responded, "My mother always told me that even if I think I can't that I should still give it a try. But first I have to believe that I can with all of my heart and mind. I believed her words as they are true; you can do anything that you put your mind to." The little boy smiled and nodded in agreement.

Soon it was time to go home and as the children stood once again admiring their work, they felt a little sad knowing tomorrow their sandcastles will be gone. Unfortunately, they will all be washed away by the waves, but they all smiled and laughed happily anyway knowing tomorrow they can try again.

The very next day, convinced that she had made some friends,
Thalia bravely stepped
one foot at a time,
right foot,
left foot,
no longer anxious in her stride,
step by step, she now walked courageously, towards the children
who were playing gleefully.

The children all smiled as Thalia approached the group.
"We are playing hide and go seek. You're it, Thalia. Cover your eyes and count to ten then start to look for us."

Thalia was overjoyed, now feeling apart of the group. This game seems interesting she thought and wasted no time getting into the groove. She began counting, "One, two, three...."

And at the end of that sunny, fun-filled day Thalia walked back to her home that stood on a hill, where she stood gazing happily at the bay. Shortly thereafter her mother appeared, smiling happily from ear to ear because she could see that her daughter was happy. Thalia embraced her mother with the warmest hug and as they walked towards their home, she told her mom quite excitedly about her day. That night Thalia gazed up at the beautifully painted sky now wishing secretly for the darkness of the night to quickly become light.

The children became the best of friends and played together every day, inseparable since that sensational day at the bay. And in the end, they all learned about forgiveness, the importance of being kind and the amazing things they can all accomplish when they make the decision to try.

also by Samantha Williams

I Am Me!
I Am Me, Too!
Women! We All Can Rise: We All Can Shine!
A to Z Positive Affirmations

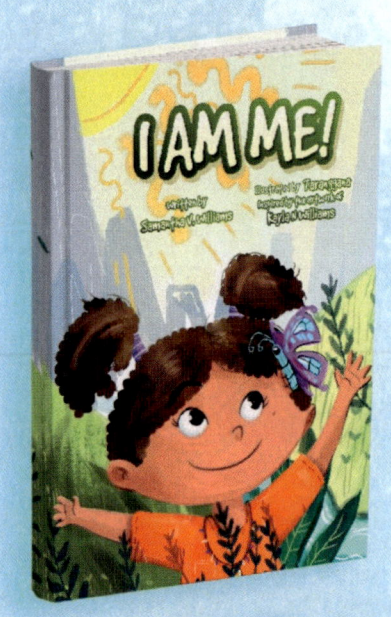

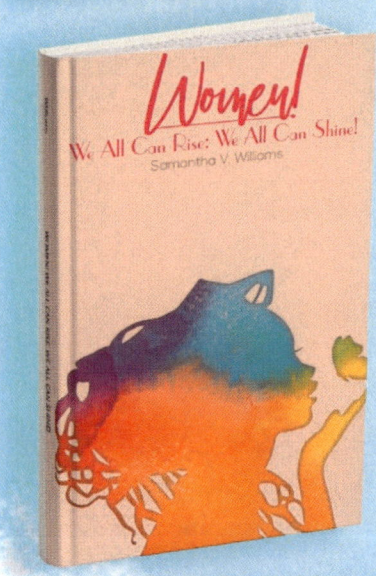

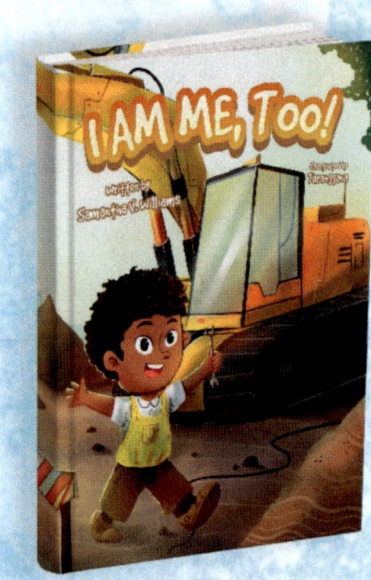

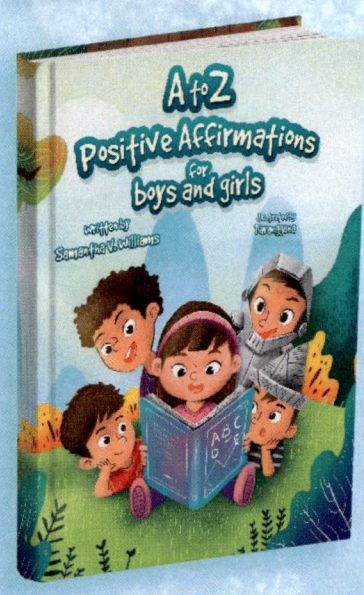

Made in United States
Orlando, FL
06 January 2024